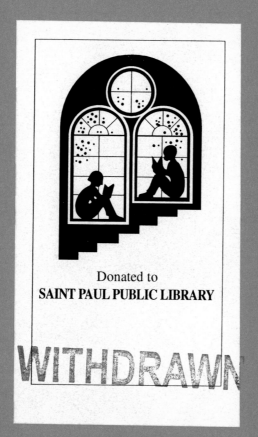

STAR WALK

edited by SEYMOUR SIMON

MORROW JUNIOR BOOKS
New York

Printed in Singapore at Tien Wah Press.

1   2   3   4   5   6   7   8   9   10

Library of Congress Cataloging-in-Publication Data
Star walk / edited by Seymour Simon.
p. cm.
Summary: A collection of poetry and photographs about stars and space.
ISBN 0-688-11887-9 (trade)—ISBN 0-688-11888-7 (library)
1. Outer space—Juvenile poetry.   2. Stars—Juvenile poetry.   3. Children's poetry, American.
4. Children's poetry, English.   [1. Outer space—Poetry.   2. Stars—Poetry.   3. American poetry.
4. English poetry.]   I. Simon, Seymour.   PS595.O87S63 1995   811.008'036—dc20   94-16643 CIP AC

Permission to use the following photographs is gratefully acknowledged: pages 3, 5, 9, 19, National Optical
Astronomy Observatories; page 7, Pekka Parviainen/Science Photo Library; page 11, Dennis Milon; pages 13,
15, 16-17, 21, 22-23, 27, 29, 32, NASA; page 25, NASA/JPL; page 31, The Association of Universities for Research in Astronomy, Inc.

Rhyme of November Stars from *Collected Poems of Sara Teasdale:* copyright © 1930 by Sara Teasdale
Filsinger, renewed 1958 by Morgan Guaranty Trust Co., reprinted by permission of Macmillan Publishing
Company. Excerpt from *The Great Bear* from *Selected Poetry,* by John Hollander: copyright © 1993 by John
Hollander, reprinted by permission of Alfred A. Knopf, Inc. *The Motion of the Earth* from *The Pot Geranium,*
by Norman Nicholson: published by Faber and Faber Ltd. and used by permission and by permission also of
David Higham Associates. *The Pleiades,* by Elizabeth Coatsworth: originally published by HarperCollins,
extensive research failed to locate the copyright holders of this work. *I Am the Moon, Song of the Stars,* and
Shooting Star from *On the Road of Stars,* selected by John Bierhorst: copyright © 1994 by John Bierhorst,
reprinted by permission of Macmillan Publishing Company. *The Flight of Apollo* from *The Poems of Stanley
Kunitz, 1928-1978,* by Stanley Kunitz: copyright © 1971, 1979 by Stanley Kunitz, reprinted by permission of
W. W. Norton & Company, Inc. *Voyage to the Moon* from *Collected Poems 1917-1982,* by Archibald MacLeish:
copyright © 1985 by The Estate of Archibald MacLeish, reprinted by permission of Houghton Mifflin Co.,
all rights reserved. Excerpt from *Mars* and excerpt from *Saturn* from *Jaguar of Sweet Laughter,* by Diane
Ackerman: copyright © 1991 by Diane Ackerman, reprinted by permission of Random House, Inc. *Letter from
Caroline Herschel (1750-1848)* from *Letters from the Floating World,* by Siv Cedering: copyright © 1984
by Siv Cedering, reprinted by permission of the University of Pittsburgh Press. *The Universe* from *New and
Selected Things Taking Place,* by May Swenson: copyright © 1963 by May Swenson, renewed 1991, used
by permission of the Literary Estate of May Swenson.

To see a world in a grain of sand
And a heaven in a wildflower,
Hold infinity in the palm of your hand
And eternity in an hour.

—William Blake

INTRODUCTION

As far back as early Native Americans such as the Passamaquoddy, and even before that, people have looked to the stars in wonder and appreciation. They wrote stories and poetry about the fixed stars and the wandering planets, the bright Sun and the changing shapes of the Moon, the glowing comets and streaking meteors. They also drew pictures of what they had seen and, in more recent times, photographed the amazing sights of space.

This book is a collection of poetry and photographs about stars and space. I have selected each poem and each photograph because it says or shows something dramatic or thoughtful about the subject. I have also chosen some prose written by Thoreau and set it as poetry. The photographs are not intended to illustrate the poems, nor are the poems intended to explain the photographs. Each is a different way of looking at the same thing, but I hope they go together and enrich each other.

Try reading each poem slowly and looking at the accompanying photograph for a long while. Allow the words of the poem and the shapes and colors of the photograph to swirl together in your mind. Then read the words again after looking at the photograph to help you broaden your appreciation of both. I hope you will write your own poetry and make your own photographs or drawings to create a new and personal connection of words and images about space.

—SEYMOUR SIMON

A computer-enhanced image of the Crab Nebula, a huge cloud of dust and gas in space

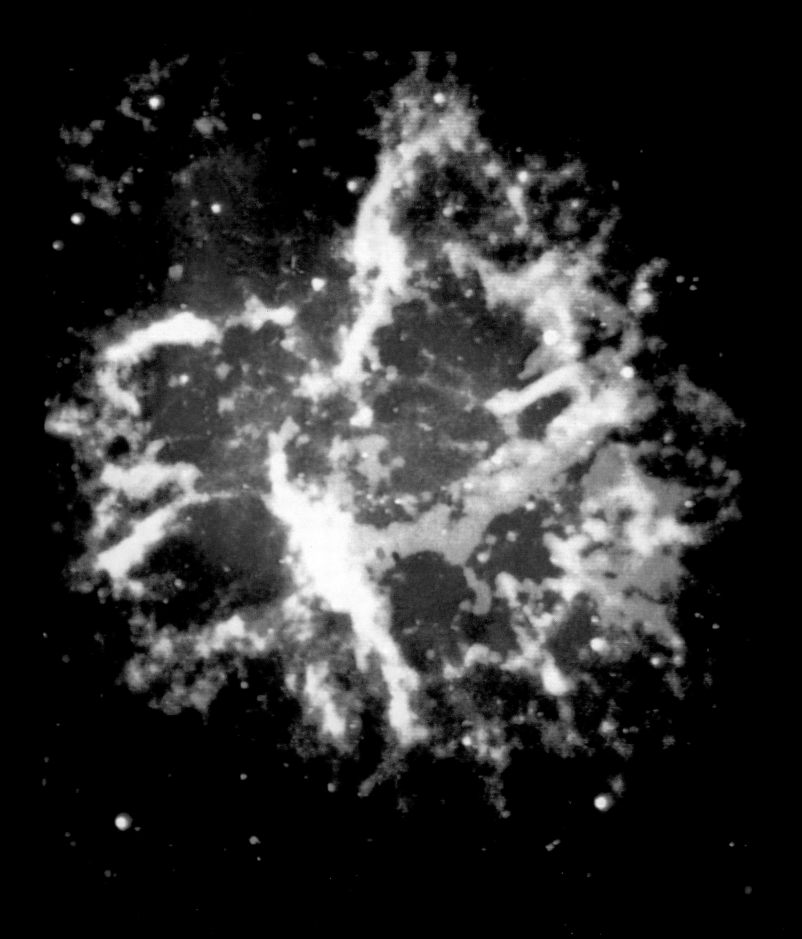

When I heard the learn'd astronomer;
When the proofs, the figures, were ranged in
   columns before me;
When I was shown the charts and the
   diagrams, to add, divide, and
   measure them;
When I, sitting, heard the astronomer,
   where he lectured with much
   applause in the lecture-room,
How soon, unaccountable, I became
   tired and sick;
Till rising and gliding out, I
   wander'd off by myself,
In the mystical moist night-air,
   and from time to time,
Look'd up in perfect silence at the stars.

—WALT WHITMAN
When I Heard the Learn'd Astronomer

Millions upon millions of stars make up the Milky Way,
a hazy band of light that stretches across the night sky.
It is a part of our Galaxy that we see from Earth.

The noiseless marching of the stars
Sweeps above me all night long;
Up the skies, over the skies,
Passes the uncounted throng,
Without haste, without rest,
From the east to the west:
Vega, Deneb, white Altair
Shine like crystals in the air,
And the lonely Fomalhaut
In the dark south, paces low.
Now the timid Pleiades
Leave the shelter of the trees,
While toward the north, mounting high,
Gold Capella, like a queen,
Watches over her demesne
Stretching toward the kingly one,
Dusky, dark Aldebaran.
Betelgeuse and Rigel burn
In their wide wheel, slow to turn,
And in the sharp November frost
Bright Sirius, with his blue light
Completes the loveliness of night.

—SARA TEASDALE
Rhyme of November Stars

The Great Nebula in the constellation Orion.
Orion contains two of the brightest stars in the night sky:
Betelgeuse and Rigel. Nearby is the brightest star in the sky:
Sirius, called the Dog Star.

. . . To understand
The signs that stars compose, we need depend
Only on stars that are entirely there
And the apparent space between them. There
Never need be lines between them, puzzling
Our sense of what is what.

The world is everything that happens to
Be true. The stars at night seem to suggest
The shapes of what might be. If it were best,
Even, to have it there (such a great bear!
All hung with stars!), there still would be no bear.

—JOHN HOLLANDER
from *The Great Bear*

The Big Dipper is part of the constellation Ursa Major, the Great Bear.
The handle of the Dipper forms the upper head and neck,
and the cup forms part of the Bear's back.

Sweet as violets to a weary heart,
Haunting as the lovely names in old tales,
Beloved as a man's own fields, are the Pleiades.

Why is one star loved and not another?
What magic is there in this little cluster
To hold the human spirit from generation to generation?

Yet there they shine, and a smile comes to men's faces,
A tenderness comes to their eyes, and voices grow quiet
Only to name the little stars, the pretty Pleiades.

—ELIZABETH COATSWORTH
The Pleiades

The Pleiades, or Seven Sisters, look to the unaided eye like six or seven rather
dim stars close together. But seen through a telescope, the Pleiades contain
several hundred stars that form a group called a star cluster.

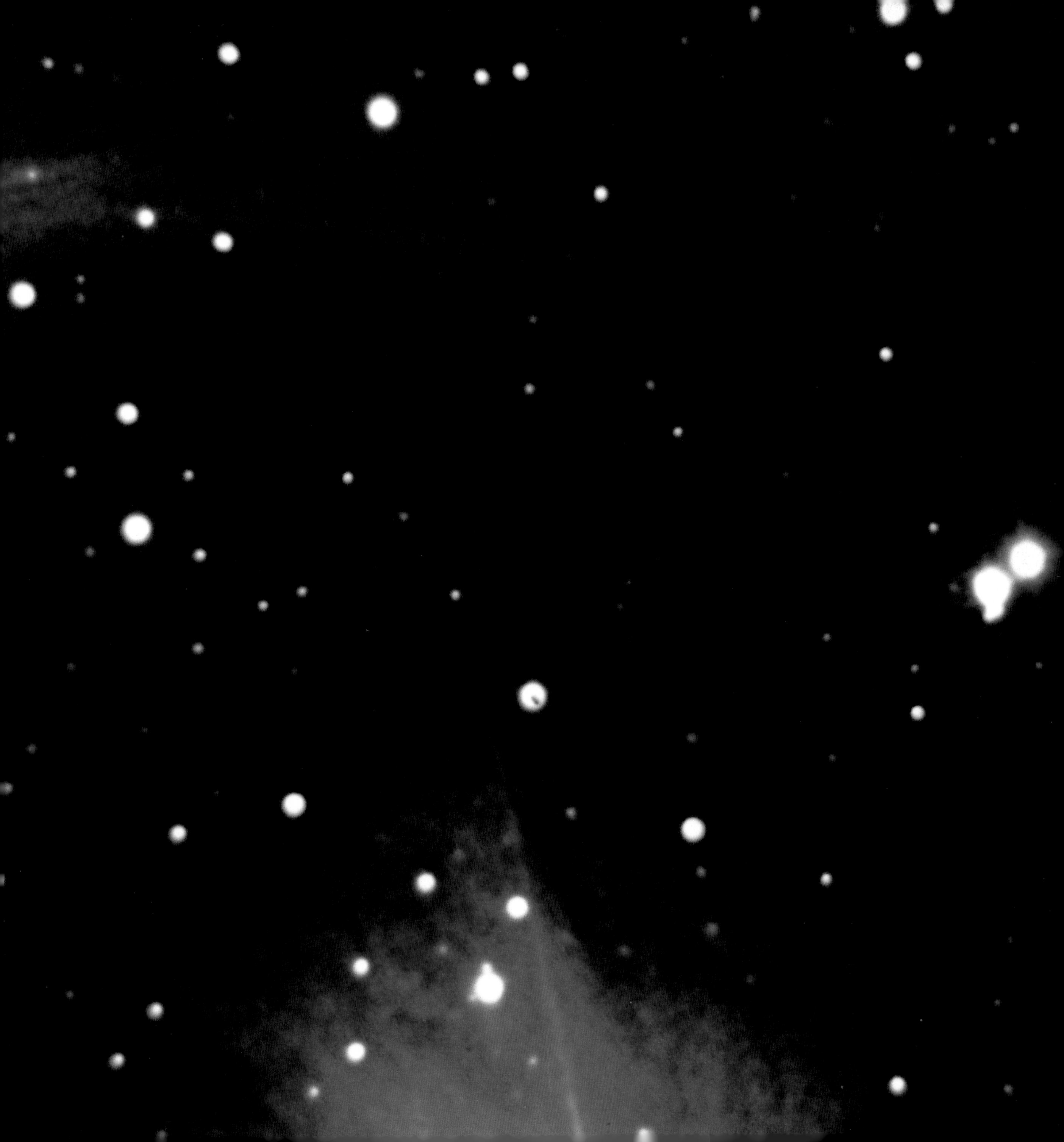

A day with sky so wide,
So stripped of cloud, so scrubbed, so vacuumed free
Of dust, that you can see
The earth-line as a curve, can watch the blue
Wrap over the edge, looping round and under,
Making you wonder
Whether the dark has anywhere left to hide.
But the world is slipping away; the polished sky
Gives nothing to grip on; clicked from the knuckle
The marble rolls along the gutter of time—
Earth, star and galaxy
Shifting their place in space.
Noon, sunset, clouds, the equably varying weather,
The diffused light, the illusion of blue,
Conceal each hour a different constellation.
All things are new
Over the sun, but we,
Our eyes on our shoes, go staring
At the asphalt, the gravel, the grass at the roadside, the doorstep,
    the doodles of snails, the crochet of mortar and lime,
Seeking the seeming familiar, though every stride
Takes us a thousand miles from where we were before.

—Norman Nicholson
The Motion of the Earth

The curve of the Earth, as seen in a
photograph taken from a space satellite.
The Sun shines brightly in the dark sky.

You star up yonder. You who gaze
up yonder. Your fingers up
yonder didn't hold very fast,
didn't knit very tight.
It fell down without touching.
Without entirely touching
against. It didn't touch.

—Inuit

Here I am
behold me
it said as it rose
I am the moon
behold me.

—Sioux

We who sing are the stars
We sing with our light
We are birds of fire
We fly through the sky
Our light is starlight
We sing on the road of spirits.

—Passamaquoddy

The bright line shows the track of a meteor.
Meteors are sometimes called falling or shooting stars,
but they are *not* stars. They are particles of rock from space
that plunge through Earth's atmosphere and burn up because of friction.

The same sun which ripens my beans
illumines at once a system of earths like ours.
The stars are the apexes of what wonderful triangles!
What distant and different beings
in the various mansions of the same universe
are contemplating the same one
at the same moment!

—HENRY DAVID THOREAU
from *Walden*

This whole earth which we inhabit
is but a point in space.
How far apart, think you,
dwell the two most distant inhabitants of yonder star,
the breadth of whose disk
cannot be appreciated by our instruments?
Why should I feel lonely?
Is not our planet in the Milky Way?

—HENRY DAVID THOREAU
from *Walden*

When I come forth in the evening,
as if from years of confinement to the house,
I see the few stars
which make the constellation of the Lesser Bear
in the same relative position—
the everlasting geometry of the stars.
How incredible to be described
are those bright points
which appear in the blue sky
as the darkness increases,
said to be other worlds,
like the berries on the hills
when the summer is ripe!

—HENRY DAVID THOREAU
from *Journal*, October 28, 1852

A fish-eye-lens view of
the arch of the Milky Way
over the night sky in Chile,
in the Southern Hemisphere.

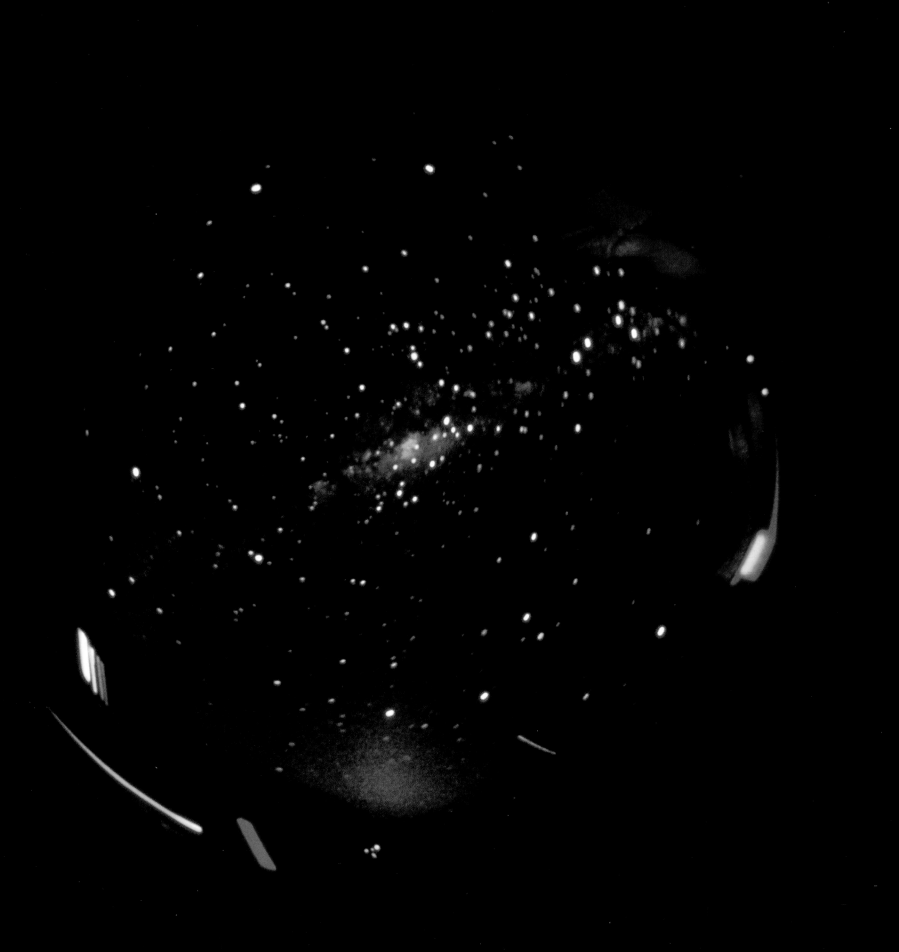

Earth was my home, but even there I was a stranger. This mineral crust.
I walk like a swimmer. What titanic bombardments in those old astral
wars! I know what I know: I shall never escape from strangeness or
complete my journey. Think of me as nostalgic, afraid, exalted. I am
your man on the moon, a speck of megalomania, restless for the leap
toward island universes pulsing beyond where the constellations set.
Infinite space overwhelms the human heart, but in the middle of
nowhere life inexorably calls to life. Forward my mail to Mars. What
news from the Great Spiral Nebula in Andromeda and the Magellanic
Clouds?

I was a stranger on earth.
Stepping on the moon, I begin
the gay pilgrimage to new
Jerusalems
in foreign galaxies.
Heat. Cold. Craters of silence.
The Sea of Tranquillity
rolling on the shores of entropy.
And, beyond,
the intelligence of the stars.

—STANLEY KUNITZ
The Flight of Apollo

Presence among us,
wanderer in our skies,
dazzle of silver in our leaves and on our
waters silver,
O silver evasion in our farthest thought—
"the visiting moon" . . . "the glimpses of the moon" . . .
and we have touched you!

From the first of time,
before the first of time, before the
first men tasted time, we thought of you.
You were a wonder to us, unattainable,
a longing past the reach of longing,
a light beyond our light, our lives—perhaps
a meaning to us.

Now our hands have touched you in your depth
of night.

Three days and three nights we journeyed,
steered by farthest stars, climbed outward,
crossed the invisible tide-rip where the floating dust
falls one way or the other in the void between,
followed that other dawn, encountered
cold, faced death—unfathomable emptiness . . .
Then, the fourth day evening, we descended,
made fast, set foot at dawn upon your beaches,
sifted between our fingers your cold sand.

We stand here in the dusk, the cold, the silence . . .
and here, as at the first of time, we lift our heads.
Over us, more beautiful than the moon, a
moon, a wonder to us, unattainable,
a longing past the reach of longing,
a light beyond our light, our lives—perhaps
a meaning to us . . .

O, a meaning!

Over us on these silent beaches the bright
earth,
      presence among us.

—ARCHIBALD MACLEISH
Voyage to the Moon

A view of the rising Earth 240 thousand miles away greets Apollo astronauts as they orbit the Moon.

Perhaps Mars
fell together once
long ago, and now,
in an ice age,
its former atmosphere
tucked discreetly
under a polar cap,
awaits the coming
of another spring.
Meanwhile the winds
chafe like emery boards,
carving rock into freeforms
and sway-backed arches.

There was a climate here
once, running water
and the blossom urge,
where sinuous dry riverbeds
stand out now
like veins on a temple.

Yet Olympus Mons,
the largest volcano
in the whole solar system,
may erupt tonight . . .
or not for a century.
I hope it will tonight.
I try to imagine
a mountain 20 miles high:
7 Alps perched
one upon the other's shoulders.

—DIANE ACKERMAN
from *Mars*

This huge Martian canyon, named Valles Marineris (for the *Mariner* spacecraft)
is more than one mile deep and three thousand miles long, about the same as
the distance from the East to the West Coast of the United States.

Millions of vest-pocket moons
hang together as rings
that loop round the planet
like a highway skirting the golden city.
Dusky bright, and god-awful sheer,
they dog the equator, never more than two miles thick:
a sprawling coral reef of tailless comets,
grinding one another
finer and finer, lolloping boulder
to dusty mote as, eddying
down through the crepiest ring,
they pour into a gassy draw.

In a seaquarium big enough
Saturn would float! lighter
than rock, or water. I marvel
it even holds together:
hydrogen-clotted ice, frozen
methane and ammonia, all lathered to a gaudy slush,
like Jupiter a bit, only colder, which may be why
the weatherworks and the lazy
cloud-roll idle as they do,
and ammonia freezes out
as a yellow blizzard, snowing
deep into the planetball.

—DIANE ACKERMAN
from *Saturn*

This photo of Saturn was taken with special color filters to make the clouds easy to see.
Saturn is made up mostly of frozen gases and liquids. The rings are pieces of ice,
some as small as your fingernail, others as big as a house.

William is away, and I am minding
the heavens. I have discovered
eight new comets and three nebulae
never before seen by man,
and I am preparing an Index to
Flamsteed's observations, together with
a catalogue of 560 stars omitted from
the British Catalogue, plus a list of errata
in that publication. William says

I have a way with numbers, so I handle
all the necessary reductions and
calculations. I also plan
every night's observation
schedule, for he says my intuition
helps me turn the telescope to discover
star cluster after star cluster.

I have helped him polish the mirrors
and lenses of our new telescope. It is
the largest in existence. Can you imagine
the thrill of turning it to some new
corner of the heavens to see
something never before seen
from earth? I actually like

that he is busy with the Royal Society
and his club, for when I finish my other work
I can spend all night sweeping
the heavens.

Sometimes when I am alone
in the dark, and the universe reveals
yet another secret, I say the names
of my long-lost sisters, forgotten
in the books that record
our science—

Aganice of Thessaly,
Hyptia,
Hildegard,
Catherina Hevelius,
Maria Agnesi

—as if the stars themselves could

remember. Did you know that Hildegard
proposed a heliocentric universe
300 years before Copernicus? that she
wrote of universal gravitation 500 years
before Newton? But who would listen
to her? She was just a nun, a woman.
What is our age, if that age was dark?
As for my name, it will also be
forgotten, but I am not accused
of being a sorceress, like Aganice,
and the Christians do not threaten to
drag me to church, to murder me, like they did
Hyptia of Alexandria, the eloquent young
woman who devised the instruments
used to accurately measure the position
and motion of

heavenly bodies.
However long we live, life is short, so I
work. And however important man becomes,
he is nothing compared to the stars.
There are secrets, dear sister, and it is
for us to reveal them. Your name, like mine,
is a song. Write soon,
Caroline

—Siv Cedering
Letter from Caroline Herschel (1750-1848)

The blue-green cloud tops of Uranus as seen from one of its largest moons, Miranda.
Uranus was discovered by Caroline Herschel's brother, William, in 1781

What
is it about,
the universe,
the universe about us stretching out?
We, within our brains,
within it,
think
we must unspin
the laws that spin it.
We think *why*
because we think
because.
Because we think,
we think
the universe about us.

But does it think,
the universe?
Then what about?
About us?
If not,
must there be cause
in the universe?
Must it have laws?
And what
if the universe
is not about us?
Then what?
What
is it about?
And what
about *us*?

—May Swenson
The Universe

The Eta-Carinae Nebula photographed through a telescope in South America.

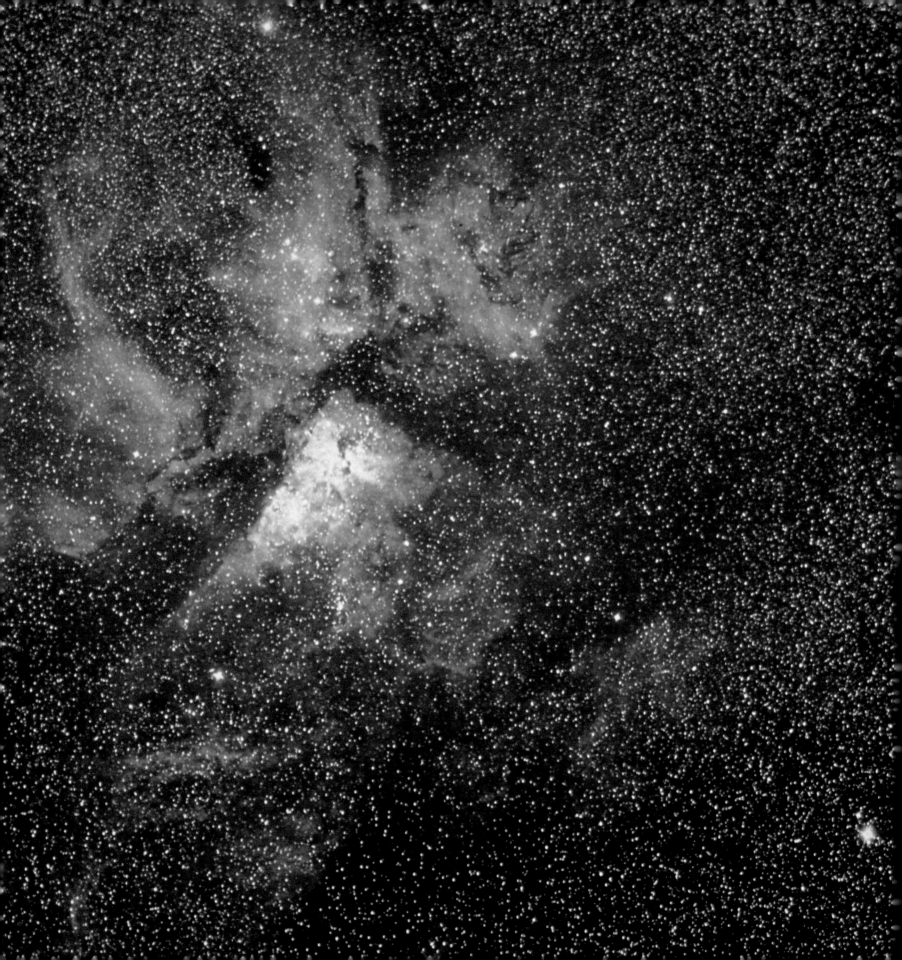

I seem to have been only a boy playing on the seashore,
and diverting myself in now and then
finding a smoother pebble or a prettier shell than ordinary,
whilst the great ocean of truth lay all undiscovered before me.

—Sir Isaac Newton

. . . a mind forever
Voyaging through strange seas of thought, alone.

—William Wordsworth on Newton
from *The Prelude*

A Gemini astronaut on a space walk, with Earth far below.